WOMEN IN RELATIONSHIPS

WOMEN IN THE WORLD™

WOMEN IN RELATIONSHIPS

ZOE LOWERY AND BETHANY BEZDECHECK

Rosen YA™

Published in 2018 by The Rosen Publishing Group, Inc.
29 East 21st Street, New York, NY 10010

First Edition

Library of Congress Cataloging-in-Publication Data

Names: Lowery, Zoe, author. | Bezdecheck, Bethany, co-author.
Title: Women in relationships / Zoe Lowery and Bethany Bezdecheck.
Description: New York : Rosen Publishing, 2018. | Series:
Women in the world | Includes bibliographical references and index.
Identifiers: ISBN 9781508174431 (library bound)
Subjects: LCSH: Interpersonal relations–Juvenile literature. | Friendship–Juvenile literature. | Women–Psychology–Juvenile literature.
Classification: LCC HM1106.L68 2018 | DDC 302–dc23

Manufactured in the United States of America

CONTENTS

INTRODUCTION

Best friends forever. BFFs. There just doesn't seem to be anything like a best buddy. Friendship is one of the most special relationships you can have in your life. Sure, family relationships are great. Many people are very close with a parent, sibling, aunt, or cousin. But we don't choose our family members. Friendship is one relationship we pick on our own,

Oprah Winfrey and Gayle King, a coanchor for *CBS This Morning*, have been fast friends for close to forty years. They met by chance when both were in their early twenties, when a Baltimore, Maryland, snowstorm forced the two together at Winfrey's home. They stayed up all night talking, and by sunrise the two had cemented a historic friendship. In 2010, Winfrey described her friend to Barbara Walters, exclaiming, "She is … the mother I never had. She is … the sister everybody would want. She is the friend that everybody deserves. I don't know a better person." She told CBS News, "In all of our years of friendship, she's always been happier for me about anything that occurred in my life.

The high-profile friendship between Gayle King and Oprah Winfrey started by chance nearly forty years ago. Our friendships are some of the few relationships we choose on our own.

When I left Baltimore and I was coming to Chicago, she was the happiest. When I got on 'The Color Purple,' she was the happiest." The supportive and encouraging friendship between the two is a wonderful example. They have even worked together, which is not always an easy thing to do, even with a best friend. Friends should be beside you through thick and thin.

Another example of good friends is comedy and acting stars Tina Fey and Amy Poehler. They met in 1993 through a Chicago improvisation group, and a friendship of performing and acting together grew through the years, including the late-night comedy show *Saturday Night Live* and several movies. In 2015 they hosted the Golden Globes together.

"It's like a good marriage," Poehler says of their friendship. "My mom always says it's very important to have people in your life who knew you when. The older you get, the more you treasure that idea of someone knowing your family and where you came from, and being around during *these* times and *these* times." And they're always supportive of one another, highlighting each other's strengths and accomplishments. "I would say that one of your greatest accomplishments, Amy Poehler, is that you have so successfully used your art and comedy as a source of positivity in the world," Fey told *People* magazine's Lindsay Kimble. "By creating … not only a positive feminist character but creating a good-hearted worldview within [*Parks and Recreation*]."

Always remember that you have love and support as you travel the sometimes rocky road through life. You have relationships with friends and family made up of people who can help steady you when you need it and bolster and highlight your strengths, just like Winfrey and King or Fey and Poehler. Every relationship takes a lot of work, but the work of a good relationship is always pretty sweet.

CHAPTER 1

A REVIEW OF RELATIONSHIPS

It's easy to immediately think of romance when the idea of relationships is brought up. We see phrases such as "committed relationship," "relationship counselor," and "same-sex relationship" that refer to couples in a romantic situation. But "romantic" refers to just one of many kinds of relationships, or the connections between people. Besides boyfriends and girlfriends, relationships can occur between siblings, coach and athlete, or coworkers, like Tina Fey and Amy Poehler, just to name a few. We have all been in all kinds of relationships beginning from the day we were born.

Tina Fey and Amy Poehler have been friends since they met in an improv group when they were both young comedians. You can meet new friends almost anywhere.

HOW TO KEEP A RELATIONSHIP HEALTHY

Here is a list of attributes required to maintain every relationship:

- **Communication.** For a relationship to survive, both parties must be aware of what the other person needs. This requires a tremendous amount of communication. To achieve clear communication, always be open and honest with the people in your relationships. This way, they'll know exactly how they ought to support you. Meanwhile, when another person takes the time to be open and honest with you, be sure to really listen and to appreciate his or her effort to communicate.
- **Shared interests and activities.** Almost all relationships exist because the people within them share a certain interest or activity. A shared activity can be anything from being on the same lacrosse team to simply living in the same household.
- **Sometimes relationships fall apart because one person ceases to be engaged in the shared activity.** Anyone who has ever changed schools,

knows what it's like to lose touch with people solely because they are no longer classmates. Still, some relationships are able to withstand changes in time, location, and interests. A friend who has moved away may still be someone with whom you speak, text, or email on a regular basis. When it comes to these particularly strong relationships, the common interest between the two parties is simply the relationship itself. Both people have enjoyed the relationship so much that they are interested in keeping it alive, no matter what changes have taken place. Social media websites, such as Facebook, make it easier to stay in touch.

- **Understanding.** No two individuals are exactly alike. Therefore, people in a relationship must work extra hard to understand each other's unique point of view. Do you ever feel like your parents just don't understand where you are coming from? There's no doubt that if they made more of an effort to understand you, your relationship would improve. Of course, all relationships work both ways. You can't very well ask someone to be understanding toward you if you aren't being understanding toward him or her.
- **Caring and kindness.** No one wants to have to put up with an unkind attitude. And if a person

(continued on the next page)

(*continued from the previous page*)

just doesn't seem to care about you, chances are, you'll stop having respect for him or her. For these reasons, caring and kindness are necessary elements for the mere existence of any relationship. Everyone deserves to be cared for and treated with kindness. If you ever find yourself in a relationship with someone who treats you poorly, the best course of action is to get out as soon as possible. Even if you still care for the other person, your well-being depends on your not staying around him or her.

- **A common goal.** Finally, for any relationship to survive, both parties must share a common goal. A relationship between a boyfriend and girlfriend, for example, can exist only if both parties want to be exclusive and not date other people. A relationship between an employee and a manager will disintegrate if one person wants to see the company do well, while the other just wants to have fun. Understanding and communication can help you tell whether you and the people in your relationships want the same thing. If you have different goals for the relationship, you'll need to work together to decide whether they can be modified. If not, the relationship won't last.

PRESERVING RELATIONSHIPS

Relationships are extremely important aspects of our lives. Think about how much you depend on friends and family, for instance. Without these relationships, you wouldn't feel as loved or secure. Your happiness depends on the well-being of your relationships, so never take them for granted. Every relationship, regardless of type, requires consistent communication, understanding, and consideration if it is to remain a part of your life.

How are relationships any fun if they require so much work? Don't worry. You should only be required to do half the work it takes to maintain a good relationship. The other person involved should provide the second half. As the relationship grows and improves, doing your part will come more naturally. Also, remember that part of a healthy relationship is being able to let go and have a little fun sometimes. Taking everything too seriously will only cause stress for you and those around you.

BEING A BETTER COMMUNICATOR

Active listening is a technique people use to become better communicators. Communication is just as much about listening as it is about talking. Listening actively helps you to understand exactly what it is the other

Remember that communication requires talking and active listening. By listening you will better understand how the other person in the relationship is feeling.

person is trying to convey. Active listening involves the following:

- Repeating what the other person has just said, but in your own words. Rephrasing shows the other person that you have been making a conscious effort to listen.
- Making eye contact with the other person while he or she is speaking, rather than exhibiting disinterest by fidgeting or focusing on something else.
- Encouraging the other person to keep communicating with you by asking positive, nonthreatening questions.
- Waiting a few moments before speaking: be sure you don't interrupt.

NAVIGATING CHOPPY WATERS: STRESSFUL RELATIONSHIPS

It is a sad fact that some people have issues that prevent them from having stable relationships. There are parents, significant others, and even authority figures, like bosses and principals, who have such a difficult time handling their own personal problems that they take their frustration out on others. If you find yourself in a relationship where you are being physically or verbally abused, it's important to find a way out. Escaping an abusive relationship can be difficult, of course, especially if the abuser is a family member.

However, getting out of an abusive relationship is a must, because staying in one can only have disastrous effects. If you are having a trying time with any sort of relationship, don't be afraid to turn to one of the following people or organizations for help.

SCHOOL COUNSELORS

School counselors are there to help you do your best. Earning good grades and nurturing your academic interests can be difficult without the support of your friends and family. School counselors are trained to help students who are dealing with troubled relationships. If you make an appointment to speak to one about the difficulties you are dealing with, you can rest assured that the counselor will keep your information confidential. He or she won't share anything you tell him or her unless the counselor feels your life is in danger.

CRISIS CENTERS

A crisis center consists of a group of highly trained individuals who assist people in coping with problems like physical abuse or drug and alcohol addiction. You can easily obtain a list of crisis centers in your area from the internet, the library, or a school counselor. Phone calls made to crisis centers are kept private, so if you place a call to one, don't worry about others finding out. A counselor may refer you to a crisis center if he or she feels your situation is an emergency. If you have contemplated suicide or if you feel your life is in danger, it is best to call a crisis center, as the people working there can make sure you receive the help you need right away.

THERAPISTS

Therapists are clinically trained professionals who work with individuals looking to improve themselves

If you feel you need more time and attention than a school counselor or crisis center can offer, consider talking to your parents about seeing a therapist.

and their relationships. Compared to school counselors and crisis centers, therapists may be in a better position to give you their full attention for an extended period of time. Some therapists work in what is known as private practice, meaning they are not affiliated with a larger organization. These therapists usually charge money for their services, and you will likely need a parent's permission to see one. However, other therapists work out of hospitals and clinics, and they may offer their assistance for free. Therapy sessions can occur between just you and the therapist, or they can occur in groups. A group therapy session is a meeting of people dealing with the same type of issue, such as coping with the loss of a loved one or escaping domestic violence. A licensed therapist usually leads these sessions, and only those who want to share that day will be requested to do so. Participating in group therapy may sound awkward or embarrassing to you, but it can

Group therapy sessions help those who want to work on their relationship as a couple, family, or other group. An objective third party might help you work things out together.

be quite helpful. If you attend a group therapy session, you will likely be relieved to meet others in your situation, and you will have the opportunity to develop new, caring relationships with these people.

Some people decide they'd like to work on their relationships together. For these motivated parties, family and couples therapy is available. Sometimes one person in a relationship has to work to convince the other person or people that going to therapy together is a good idea. This is because many people fear that receiving therapy means they aren't capable of solving their own problems. What these people don't realize is that it often takes an objective third party to help people see a relationship clearly, especially when strong personal feelings are at play.

Seeking outside help with your relationships is nothing to be ashamed of. It takes a strong, determined person to put forth this type of effort.

You can't get out of negative relationships too fast, but it's important to cultivate those that are positive. Make time for these relationships and give them your attention, whether they are with a teacher or your friend down the street. We all feel bad when we're ignored or taken for granted. Keep reading to learn about how to take care of all kinds of relationships and, especially, your important relationship with yourself.

MYTHS AND FACTS

MYTH: A good relationship shouldn't require any work; getting along should come naturally to the people involved.

FACT: All relationships require work. It is impossible for any two people to see things in the exact same way. Therefore, it's important that both parties in a relationship work hard on communicating effectively.

MYTH: The actions of parents, teachers, and other authority figures must never be questioned.

FACT: No one, no matter what their age or stature, should have to put up with a hurtful relationship. If a parent, teacher, or other authority figure is showing you disrespect, do not let that person's behavior slide. Explain the situation to a trustworthy adult, and allow him or her to help you decide what is to be done.

MYTH: If you love your partner, you should be willing to take your relationship to a physical level.

FACT: Just because you care for someone doesn't mean you should be ready to engage with him or her in sexual activity. The decision to have sex involves more than just emotions, and it should never be taken lightly. If someone is pressuring you to have sex, know that in doing this, he or she is being anything but loving.

CHAPTER 2

FAMILY TIES

The famous saying is true: You can choose your friends but not your relatives. It's simple. We can decide who we are friends with, based on who we like. But we're stuck with our relatives, regardless of whether we have much in common with them.

This notion may seem gloomy at times, but being stuck with someone isn't all bad. Remember, while friends come and go, family is forever. No matter where you are or what life brings your way, your family members will be a part of your life. Family love is truly precious because it is unconditional. Both because of and in spite of this, it should not be taken for granted.

From talking with your friends, you probably know it's not unusual for family to get on a teenager's nerves.

Sometimes your family members might really get on your nerves, but always try to think about how you act around them and treat them, too.

Family members can be embarrassing, nagging, and annoying, and the worst part is, they're always around! But have you ever asked yourself how you might come across to your family? Are you always kind and courteous, or do stress and irritability sometimes make you difficult to be around? Remember, relationships work both ways, and it's not fair to ask others to change their behavior toward you unless you're willing to do the same for them.

You may have heard the phrase, "Someone needs to be the bigger person." When people are at odds, one of them needs to be able to step up and make things right. Otherwise, the anger and hurt feelings will go on forever. If you are the bigger person in your family, your parents and siblings will be motivated to follow your good example. In addition, they will be impressed by your actions and will therefore pay you more respect. Earning respect from your family is very important. When people respect you, they are more likely to trust you to make your own decisions.

KEEPING THE PEACE

Of course being the first person to take a step toward household peace is easier said than done. When your parents are quizzing you about your grades and complaining that you never help out around the house, chances are you'll feel more like screaming than being the bigger person. Thankfully, there are some useful tips and tricks for getting through such initial frustration.

First, see it from their side. Different members of a family see things completely different ways. While this alone can cause disagreements, it's forgetting this simple fact itself that keeps people from making amends. For effective communication, families must first recognize that each member has a unique point of view.

Because your parents or guardians care so much about your well-being, they can seem preoccupied with things like your schoolwork and safety. To them, keeping a close eye on these matters means being a cautious and compassionate caregiver. However, you might find your parents' prudent actions overbearing, obnoxious, and unnecessary. In your mind, you might feel you're too old to need someone watching over you constantly. You may also feel your parents are being unsympathetic by thinking only of your curfew and grades, while ignoring those things that make you truly happy, like your social life and extracurricular interests.

With such different viewpoints, you and your family members may never completely see eye to eye. First, you can at least try to understand one another's perspective. If your parents are able to see how you can be negatively affected by their actions, they may think

Try to resist lashing out at your family members, even when they stress you out. They are more likely to listen to you and take you seriously if you remain calm.

twice before doing something that could upset you. Meanwhile, you'll be less likely to get so angry with them once you recognize that their nagging ways are only motivated by compassion.

Second, resist anger. When family members cause you stress, your first reaction may be to fight back. Such a reaction is perfectly natural, as fighting makes people feel better by allowing them to release their negative emotions. In the long run, however, anger can only make a situation worse.

Most adults see an angry outburst as being a sign of immaturity. Therefore, if you react to what you feel is an unfair situation by yelling at your parents or giving them the silent treatment, the only thing you'll prove to them is that you're too immature to be taken seriously. While everyone deserves to be listened to, the only way your parents or guardians will really take in what you have to say is if you present your thoughts in a calm, respectful manner.

And last, learn the art of compromise. A family is not a dictatorship, so no one person should be allowed to have his or her way all the time. Of course, most people prefer things to go their way, and some will start arguments in an effort to get what they want. To prevent such fights from impairing your relationships, it's important to learn the art of compromise.

Compromising means coming to an agreement through which both parties get their way in exchange for a small sacrifice. As an example, let's say you and your older sister both want to use the family car. Your sister wants to drive to the library to return some books, then go to the mall to pick up a new cell phone she's been saving her money for. You, however, have a friend coming over and would like the car so you can drive to the grocery store to buy the ingredients to make a stir-fry. Neither of your schedules permits you to use the car at a later time.

Instead of causing hurt feelings by fighting over the car, you and your sister can compromise by riding together. If the two of you don't have time to complete all four tasks, you can each select the one that is most important to you and save the other for a later date. Doing this means neither of you will completely get your way, but you can both agree that it's better than one of you not being able to use the car at all.

If you and your sister both need to use the family car at the same time, talk it out and come to an agreement, such as doing your errands together.

BRIDGING THE AGE GAP

Disagreements between family members are often the result of age differences. This can be especially obvious when dealing with your parents. As a teenager, you're at a time in your life when it is important to you to feel independent. Meanwhile, your parents are at an age when their biggest concern is your safety. The result is that while you want to make decisions on your own, your parents want to know exactly what you're doing and where you are at all times. Needless to say, these different desires do not mix.

Age differences between siblings can also be a cause for family arguments. Younger siblings might admire their older siblings and look for reasons to be around them, while older siblings might want their space.

People of very different ages can't be expected to see situations the exact same way. Therefore, everyone

If you and your younger brother are several years apart in age, it may be difficult to see his viewpoint. Try to give him a chance to express his feelings.

in your family needs to take extra steps to understand one another's points of view. Be the bigger person and remind your family members that it's natural for you to have your differences, and encourage them to allow everyone the opportunity to express their opinions.

As you grow older, you may find that your family relationships improve. An older brother who once found you a nuisance may discover that now that you've matured, he has more in common with you and wouldn't mind hanging out with you occasionally. One day when you move out on your own and no longer have to answer to your parents or guardians, you may find you are less annoyed by them. Until these changes occur, however, maintaining good family relationships will require working to see things from other family members' perspectives, swallowing your anger, and learning to compromise.

X AND Y: THE GENERATIONS

You, your parents, and your grandparents are all from different generations. A generation is a group of individuals born around the same period of time. Different generations have grown up in very different ways. If your grandparents are between the ages of sixty and eighty, they were your age during a time when people of different races were not considered equal in the United States. They also endured the Cold

War, a period of tension between the United States and the Soviet Union that caused great levels of suspicion and anxiety. If your parents were born in the 1960s or 1970s, they're known as members of Generation X. This generation grew up in very stable times compared to those of their parents. As teenagers, members of Generation X rebelled against the more conservative ideologies of the past. Did you know your generation is referred to as Generation Y? What do you think it will be remembered for? It's up to you and your peers to make sure your generation is looked upon positively.

Differences in generations naturally cause differences in personalities and outlooks on life. They are, therefore, another source of tension within families. However, these differences don't have to cause conflict, as long as families remember to keep them in mind when communicating.

YOUR EXTENDED FAMILY

Family relationships are more difficult to manage when it comes to your immediate family—your parents and siblings. Getting along with extended family—aunts, uncles, cousins, and grandparents—is usually easier. This is because these family members aren't around you as much and are therefore less likely to get on your nerves. Plus, you don't need to worry about constantly seeking their approval. They don't have control over your actions the way your parents do. At the same time, if you're like most people, you're actually closer to your immediate family than you are to your extended family. The reason for this is, because you don't see your extended family as often, you probably know less about them.

Even though you may not see your extended family members every day, it's a good idea to work on building these relationships. Solid relationships with extended family members can be very rewarding. They will help you to better enjoy large family get-togethers, and if you ever find yourself in a situation in which you need to depend on an aunt, uncle, or grandparent, you will feel more comfortable doing so if you are close to that person.

It's easy to improve relationships with extended family. Your extended family members have watched you grow up, and for this reason alone, they are invested in your well-being. It is inevitable that they will appreciate your making an effort to get to know them better. There are a few ways you can become closer to your extended family. For example, a couple of times a year, send a handwritten note to extended family members who do not live nearby. Older relatives especially enjoy handwritten cards, which they probably rarely receive since the invention of email. Thank-you notes for birthday or holiday gifts are the perfect opportunity for showing your extended family you care.

Relationships with family members you might not see all the time, such as grandparents or aunts and uncles who live far away, are still important and worth developing.

Another way to become closer to your extended family is to learn about your genealogy, or family tree. Discovering where you came from and who your ancestors were is always interesting. Ask your extended family members for help. They will be able to tell you about relatives you are too young to have known.

Or ask your grandparents (or great-grandparents, -aunts, or -uncles) what life was like when they were your age. It's fun to imagine your grandparents as teenagers, and older people enjoy reminiscing about their youth.

STEPFAMILIES

In addition to immediate and extended family, many people have stepfamilies. With the divorce rate on the rise, more than half of today's teenagers have stepparents. These relationships can be particularly stressful. If one of your parents remarries, you may feel it's unfair to be expected to treat a strange, new adult like one of the family. No one is asking that you love your new stepparent more than you love your biological mother or father, though. The most that is expected from you in dealing with a stepparent is that you show that person respect.

Adjusting to stepfamilies is difficult for adults, too. Stepparents never mean for their current marriage

FAMILY ACROSS THE GLOBE

In some cultures, it's common for immediate and extended family to live together. For example, in China and Korea, it's traditional for adult sons to bring their wives to live with them and their parents and grandparents. When daughters marry, they move in with the extended families of their husbands.

As more people from around the world are moving from rural areas to live in big cities, the number of extended families living together continues to decrease. At the same time, however, it is consistently common for the elderly to move in with their sons and daughters once they can no longer care for themselves. This is becoming increasingly common in the United States.

to hurt anyone. Their main objective is simply enjoying time with their chosen life partner. However, they can't help but worry that their new stepsons or stepdaughters will resent them. If you have a stepmother or stepfather, it may help you to remember that he or she is probably just as confused and concerned by the relationship as you are. If the two of you find a way to get along, it will be a great relief to both of you, as well as to your remarried parent.

FAMILY FOREVER

Of course most teens would rather spend time with friends instead of family. Friends are about the same age and they get along because they have so much in common. It's possible, however, that you may actually come to appreciate hanging out at home. With a bit of extra effort, you can make family relationships better. Your family is your family forever, and those ties are joys that can last a lifetime.

CHAPTER 3

THE GIFT OF FRIENDSHIP

Most teens depend on their friends. Friends know you better than almost anyone. Usually, younger siblings are too immature to relate to teenagers, and most adults no longer recall how it felt to be young. So having a solid group of friends is important for everyone.

Most people, no matter how old they are, look for the same qualities in a friend. These qualities include the following:

- **Loyalty:** A loyal friend would never do anything that might hurt you. A loyal friend values your friendship and understands that in order to maintain it, she must be honest and true to you.

- **Kindness:** Of course, kindness is a necessary quality in a friend.

Your good friends should be loyal, kind, respectful, and empathetic. They should also have common interests and some of the same personality traits as you do.

In order to be happy, you must be surrounded by caring and compassionate people, not people who are rude or couldn't care less about your feelings.

- **Respect:** Everyone deserves respect, especially a good friend. No matter how close two people become, they should never take each other for granted. A long-lasting friendship means long-lasting respect.

- **Empathy:** An empathetic friend is someone who understands your emotions. When you're going through a tough time, she will sympathize with you and help you to feel better. When you succeed, she will be happy for you and help you celebrate. A friend with whom you can share your ups and downs is a friend with empathy.

- **Common interests:** It's fun to have friends who share

Any time you go someplace new, whether you move to a different city or join a new club, you'll have to make friends. It's perfectly normal if this stresses you out.

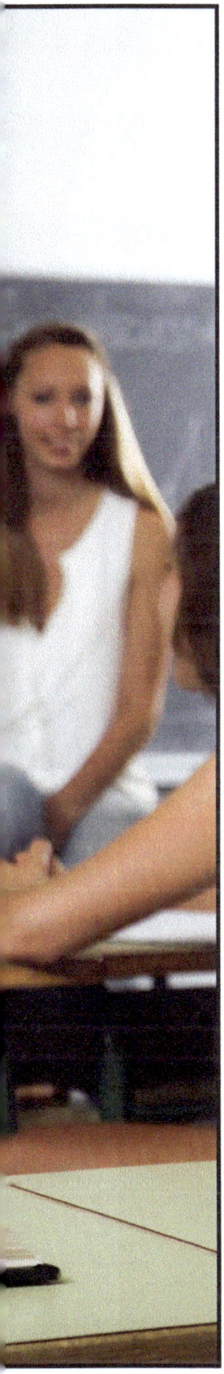

your interests. You can talk to them about the things that excite you and take part in activities together.

- **Similar personality traits:** People with similar personalities tend to get along better because they find it easier to relate to each other. Therefore, it's typical for good friends to have similar personalities.

The writer Khalil Gibran said, "Friendship is always a sweet responsibility, never an opportunity." If you want your friends to possess the aforementioned qualities, you need to make sure you possess them, as well. Of course, you can't be expected to have control over your interests or personality traits, but you need to be respectful and kind toward your friends if you want them to treat you the same.

FINDING NEW FRIENDS

Moving to a new town, switching to a new school, or joining a new organization like the track team or vocal ensemble means having to make new friends. If you find this

If you're anxious about talking to new people, remember that many people find this stressful. It may be hard at first, but you'll be glad you made the effort.

concept stressful, you're not alone. Even adults experience anxiety over making new friends. When you're the "new person," you worry about not fitting in and figure that since everyone else already has a group of friends, they won't be interested in including one more person. Of course, such a defeatist attitude won't make you friends. It's better to recognize that in order to assist your social life, you may have to step outside of your comfort zone. In other words, you'll have to do a few things that may feel uncomfortable at first, like asking a group of girls if you can sit with them at lunch or striking up a conversation with someone whose company you think you'd enjoy. You may feel nervous and awkward doing these things in the beginning, but once you've successfully formed some new friendships, you'll wonder what you were once so scared about. The truth is, everyone is interested in building new friendships, and most people will be able to sympathize with your situation. So don't be afraid of assertively seeking friends. You'll thank yourself later on.

THE RIGHT AND WRONG REASONS

It's not uncommon for teens to choose friends for the wrong reasons. More often than not, these reasons have to do with popularity. As a teenager, popularity can seem immensely important. You are working to create an identity for yourself through the clothes you wear, the music you listen to, and the people you hang out with, and you are relying on your peers to tell you whether this identity is acceptable. The more popular you are, the more you can rest assured that others approve of your persona.

Because forging an identity can be frustrating, some teens choose to rely on others to create one for them. They seek out friends who are already popular because they know associating themselves with these people will make them seem cooler. Of course, in doing this, they are denying themselves the

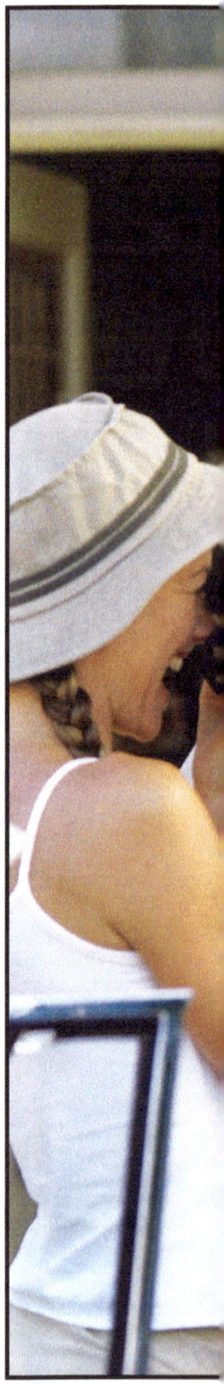

Some friends may take part in activities that make you uncomfortable, such as smoking. You can still be friends, but be ready to stand up for your own beliefs.

opportunity to get to know their true selves. This isn't a good idea because while friends may come and go, you're with yourself for life.

If you choose your friends for popularity rather than loyalty, kindness, and respect, you can't expect to have a very good support system. Someone who cares more about your social status than about your feelings isn't likely to help you up when you're down. At times, it may seem like popularity will make you happy, but if being popular means not having true friends, it's more likely to make you miserable.

SORTING OUT DISAGREEMENTS

Even if you keep the aforementioned advice in mind, you will never completely avoid having disagreements with your friends. Everyone has disagreements from time to time, no matter how good they are at handling relationships. If you and your friends do end up in an argument, there are some ways in which you can help to put things to rest:

1. **Force yourself to listen.** No matter how wrong you think a friend may be, it's only fair to allow her

to share her feelings. The only way you can expect her to listen to you is if you actively listen to her.

2. **Change your shoes.** In the previous chapter, you learned about how putting yourself in a family member's shoes can help to end a disagreement. The same trick works with friends. If you look at a situation from a friend's point of view, you may be surprised to find she has a valid point. In addition, once she sees how willing you are to consider her side of things, she'll be compelled to do the same for you.

3. **Keep it private.** Asking mutual friends to take sides in an argument is equivalent to asking for trouble. Involving more people than necessary in a disagreement will only cause it to grow out of hand, and friends will rightfully see you as disloyal if you work to turn others against them. Having a third party intervene in a dispute can be helpful, but only if that person is objective and experienced, like a school counselor.

Solving problems in a mature and healthy manner will help make your friendships stronger. Your friends will recognize that you care enough about them to do whatever it takes to keep your relationship positive.

DEALING WITH DISPUTES AND BECOMING DISTANT

The friends you make for the right reasons have the potential to stay with you for a lifetime. However, it's important to understand that sometimes even the best of friends can grow apart. People change as they grow older. They develop different interests, move to different areas, and come to want different things from life. If you should find yourself growing distant from a friend, recognize that no one is to blame. Such occurrences are perfectly natural, and there's no good reason to get upset over this type of situation. Also remember that nothing can take away the good memories you have from when you and your friend were closer, and just because a friendship changes, it doesn't mean it's over. Treasure your friendships, both for what they were and for what they are today.

Just as it's normal for friends to grow apart, it's normal for friends to have disagreements. Have you ever been upset with a friend for one of the following reasons?

YOU'RE CRUSHING ON THE SAME PERSON

It's a given that friends with similar interests and personality traits will be attracted to the same type of people. Of course, this can lead to some unfriendly

You and your friend may be interested in the same person. In that case it might be better if neither of you pursues him or her. Don't risk your friendship!

competition. What will happen if you and a friend of yours end up liking the same boy or girl? Many girls respond to this sort of predicament by trying to outdo each other and hurling accusations back and forth. In the end, it may not be that either of them has won the person's approval, but one thing is for certain: their friendship has been destroyed.

What is the appropriate way, then, to deal with this type of situation? Should you simply swallow your true feelings and let your friend go after the person you like? If doing so would cause you pain and resentment, then the answer is a definite no. You need to be fair to yourself, as well as fair to your friend. Because it's unlikely that your friend would stand by and just watch you pursue the boy or girl either, there is but one solution to this common conundrum. You must suggest to your friend that neither of you goes after your mutual crush.

Undoubtedly, you and your friend will have a difficult time putting aside your love interest. However, it's important to recognize that no crush is worth losing a true friend. If you choose a romantic relationship over a friendship and the romantic relationship should come to an end, you'll find yourself wishing your friend was still around to support you.

A NEW FRIEND IS GETTING IN THE WAY

You may become upset if a friend of yours is spending less time with you after meeting someone else.

It never feels good when a friend meets and starts spending some of his or her time with someone else, but everyone has lots of friends.

Whether this "someone else" is a boyfriend, girlfriend, or another friend, it's possible that you'll worry your friend prefers him or her to you. Jealousy can often lead to anger, so this type of situation has the potential to turn pretty nasty.

If you're ever faced with this type of problem, you must first remind yourself that no one can "steal" a friend. A friend is not something you own, like a cell phone or a piece of jewelry. A friend is an independent human being who has the right to spend time with whoever she pleases. Also, just because a friend enjoys another person's company doesn't mean she cares less about you. No one can have too many friends. There's always room for everyone, and if you remain loyal, kind, and empathetic, you won't be canceled out.

Of course, being a true friend does mean making sure you have time enough for everyone. It's fine to hang out with different people every so often, but if you haven't seen a certain friend for quite some time, he or she may have a right to be upset with you. Make sure to give all your friends a piece of your time, and ask them to do the same for you.

PEER PRESSURE TAKES OVER

Have you ever heard the phrase "the more, the merrier"? This notion can be what dictates peer pressure. People sometimes feel better about the bad things they're doing if other people are doing them, too. For example,

A real friend understands that you have your own convictions. If a friend tries to pressure you, take a step back and see if this person is a true friend.

a teenager who starts smoking cigarettes might feel guilty about her new habit, but if her friends start doing it with her, she'll at least feel she's not alone.

As a teenager, you're at an age when experimenting with harmful things like drinking, smoking, and drugs is, unfortunately, commonplace. Some teens feel that by doing things they shouldn't, they are letting the world know they are their own bosses. At the same time, however, they're putting their grades, health, and friendships in jeopardy. So much for being good bosses to themselves!

If you find yourself being pressured by a friend, you may worry that if you don't do what he or she asks, you'll lose that companionship. What you may not realize, however, is that a true friend would never ask you to do something to hurt yourself. Because holding on to a false friend is pointless, there's no reason for you to feel bad about saying "no" to peer pressure.

It could be that a friend of yours becomes the victim of peer pressure. If this should happen, try not to think of her as a bad person. Not everyone is strong enough to avoid doing something unhealthy in an effort to fit in. However, this doesn't mean you should hold your tongue while your friend races down the wrong path. A good friend should want what's best for the other person, and in this case, what's best for your friend is that you let her know she's making a big mistake.

Ending any friendship in which someone forces you to do things you don't want to do or disrespects you will make you a much happier person. It's not easy to dissolve a friendship, but remember that you cannot be friends with everyone. If you are strong enough to spend your time with people who genuinely like and respect you, you'll be a whole lot healthier and much better off.

CHAPTER 4

MATTERS OF THE HEART

You and your peers are at a time when many of you may be embarking upon your first romantic relationships. These relationships are different from others in that they exist exclusively between two people. Usually, these two people possess a unique emotional connection and mutual desire for each other. Many teenage girls look forward to having a boyfriend or girlfriend so that they can take part in this special and thrilling experience. However, it's unnecessary to obsess over finding a significant other. Many young women who have been part of a couple will tell you that being single can be just as much fun. Being in a

Everyone communicates in different ways, so getting to know someone, especially in a new romantic relationship, means learning how that person shares his or her feelings.

romantic relationship does have its advantages, but it also requires hard work and certain sacrifices.

Dating means learning to understand other people. This task is never easy. Not everyone is going to relate to your point of view. Many of the problems that arise between couples have to do with the very different ways in which women and men communicate. For example, some girls worry that their partners don't care about them because they rarely volunteer to share their feelings. What these girls forget is that, by nature, some people tend to be less emotionally expressive than others. Therefore, when your significant other doesn't offer to tell you exactly how he or she is feeling, it doesn't necessarily mean they're heartless. Most likely, they're just more reserved.

Whether they're made up of men or women, couples need to make an effort to understand each other. Since you can't expect your partner to react to things the same way you do, you'll have to get to know his or her behavior well enough in order to really know what's on his or her mind. A good partner will do the same for you. Your significant other will want to get to know you on such a level that he or she can tell how you're feeling just by looking at you. Achieving this kind of closeness takes time, but working toward it is a great exercise in building the strongest of relationships.

When it comes to dating, boys are traditionally the ones who do the asking out. This is no longer the case. In the twenty-first century, anyone can ask another person out on a date. In fact, doing so will only be beneficial to your dating record. Right away, the number of dates you go on will increase dramatically. You may think that all the people who are interested in you have already asked you out. This is never actually the case. Some people are far too shy to approach you, and they will be relieved if you approach them instead. The only way to find out who these shy people are is to ask them out and see what they say.

TEEN DATING IN THE DIGITAL AGE

Digital devices and social media are now the name of the game in teenage dating. According to an article by Amanda Lenhart, Monica Anderson, and Aaron Smith, a survey by the Pew Research Center throughout 2014 and 2015 of 1,000 American teens from ages 13 to 17 revealed how they approach dating.

- 55 percent showed their interest in others in real life.
- 50 percent friended their interest on social media.
- 47 percent flirted by "liking" or commenting on items their interest had posted.

(continued on the next page)

Although digital devices can be a great way to communicate, the ease of keeping in touch is often abused in the dating world.

(*continued from the previous page*)

- 85 percent expected their partner to check in once a day or even more often.
- 11 percent wanted to connect with their partner hourly.
- 10 percent have shared either flirty or sexy photos or videos featuring themselves.
- 25 percent reported blocking someone because of unwelcome attention.
- More than 25 percent said internet posts had resulted in jealousy or uncertainty regarding their relationship.
- 20 percent reported having their text messages read by their partner without permission.
- 13 percent reported being forced by their partners to share their passwords.
- 27 percent had used text messages to break up with someone (approximately the same as those who had done so by phone).
- 14 percent had experienced their partner or ex saying nasty things about them either on the internet or by cell phone following the breakup.
- 10 percent admitted to accessing the social media accounts of a partner or ex.
- 10 percent had altered or deleted the profile of their partner or ex.

WILL YOU GO OUT WITH ME?

You may be hesitant to address your crush, for fear of rejection. If so, you're not alone. Everyone—even the most popular person in school—agonizes over being rejected. Allowing this fear to cripple you, however, will do nothing to improve your love life. While you can expect to be met with rejection once in a while, the only way to get someone to say yes to a date is to ask someone out in the first place.

It is important not to take rejection too personally. Teens don't always turn down dates just because they don't like the other person. Sometimes they're simply too nervous to give dating a shot. Other times, they may be dealing with a difficult breakup and aren't quite ready to date again just yet. If you get rejected, don't waste your time asking yourself why it happened. You'll probably never know the real reason. Instead, congratulate yourself on being brave enough to have taken a risk. If you are able to successfully face rejection, you won't be as afraid to ask for the things you want out of life and will consequently become more accomplished.

Once you do start dating, be careful not to let the intoxication of having a love life cloud your vision. Have you ever had a friend who started dating and then suddenly seemed to disappear? Some people become so wrapped up in having a significant other

If someone declines your request to go out, there may be a reason why he or she said no, and it may have nothing to do with you at all!

that they lose sight of everything else around them, including their friends. No matter how enamored you are of someone, try not to become a "vanishing friend." Should your romantic relationship go sour, you'll want your friends by your side, and they'll be reluctant to support you if they feel you've been ignoring them.

FLIRTATION AND FAITH

Most Western cultures are fairly lenient when it comes to teens spending time with the opposite sex. In mainly Muslim countries, such as Iran for example, this type of interaction is looked down upon, especially if a parent or guardian isn't present. Some Muslim teens living in Western countries have a hard time reconciling their religious backgrounds with their social lives. For example, if their friends are going to the movies or a party, they won't be able to go along if teens of the opposite sex will be present. Some Muslims do not date at all. In the Jewish tradition, dating is not for fun. It has a purpose: to select a lifetime mate. Many cultures still do not approve of homosexual relationships, so lesbian, gay, bisexual, or transgendered (LGBT) people may have a difficult time.

Another thing you must keep an eye on while dating is your sense of self. Some young women make the mistake of allowing their romantic relationships to define them. They forget about their own interests and needs in order to concentrate completely on those of their significant other. Don't disrespect yourself by abandoning your individuality. You are a special person with her own hopes, dreams, and interests, and these things must never be compromised in the name of a relationship.

GOING SOLO

It could be that at this time, you're just not interested in having a boyfriend or girlfriend. You either have too many other things on your plate or you'd rather not have to deal with the drama that sometimes comes with having a significant other. Such an outlook is perfectly healthy. It's good to have a positive attitude about being single. Not having a partner gives you more time to focus on yourself and your needs. Unfortunately, many girls have the idea that life won't be complete until they are dating someone. This misconception not only brings down their self-esteem, it also prompts them to settle for less of a person than they deserve.

If you catch yourself pining for a partner simply because you're lonely or depressed, stop it right there! A significant other is not a cure for either of these

Sometimes we're too busy with school or other activities to carve out time for a special someone. Spending time alone can be extremely healthy.

afflictions. In fact, the only way you can have a happy and healthy romantic relationship is if you are first happy and healthy on your own. Depending entirely upon a girlfriend or boyfriend for your sense of self-worth means that once you break up, your confidence level will at once be at a dangerous low.

When in a romantic relationship, it is vital that you take things slowly. Your romantic relationship will become much stronger if you take the time to really get to know the other person before doing things like kissing or having sex. Many teens move from one level of a romantic relationship to the next far too quickly. Girls sometimes worry that if they don't get physical with their partners right away, they'll be dumped.

They forget that being with someone who cares about them on merely a physical level isn't worth their time. A healthy romantic relationship should be more about caring and compassion than sexual activity. If your significant other is pressuring you to do things you aren't yet comfortable with, don't allow yourself to give in. He or she will be more likely to respect you if he sees that you value your body enough to move at your own pace. If someone tells you differently, it's more than safe to assume that the person isn't right for you, or anyone else, for that matter.

Earlier, you read about the attributes that are necessary for the survival of any healthy relationship. One of these attributes was having a common goal. It's crucial to ask yourself from time to time whether you and your partner seem to want the same thing out of your relationship. If you're ever not sure of the answer, the two of you may want to have a talk. Staying

In a healthy relationship, both partners will respect one another's decisions. If one of you isn't ready to move forward sexually, the other should be understanding.

in a relationship only makes sense if both parties are moving toward the same goal.

BREAKING UP IS HARD TO DO

Unfortunately, most romantic relationships do come to an end. If you're in a committed relationship, it's important to make sure you're with the person who's best for you. No relationship is completely without problems, and it's normal for you and your partner to have disagreements once in a while. However, there are some very specific signs that point to a romantic relationship being ready to come to a close.

YOU WANT DIFFERENT THINGS

Again, there's no point in prolonging a relationship in which there is no common goal. If one of you wants a long-term commitment and the other thinks you should consider your relationship no more than a summer fling, it's best to put an end to things on the spot. You'll never see eye to eye on the matter, and sticking things out will only prolong an inevitable bad breakup.

YOUR FEELINGS HAVE CHANGED

It's common for a couple to lose the romantic feelings they once had for each other. People grow apart from their significant others, just as they grow apart from their friends. If you find yourself losing interest in your partner, there's no need to feel guilty about things. Simply be honest about what you're feeling and bring up the possibility of the two of you parting ways. You may be tempted to stay in the relationship in an effort to see whether your romantic feelings come back to you, but it's unlikely that this will happen. Once you lose romantic interest in a person, it's almost impossible to naturally regain that interest. The best thing to do in this type of situation is to move on and not spend any additional time being a part of something that no longer excites you.

YOU ARGUE ALL THE TIME

No two people get along all the time, but if you and your boyfriend are fighting more than you are enjoying each other's company, something is amiss in your relationship. Constant quarreling doesn't mean that one of you is a negative person or that you should try harder to make things work. Usually, it just means that the two of you have grown apart and are therefore no longer able to relate to each other. It's best for this realization to lead to a breakup, as sticking with a relationship in which all you do is argue will only prolong the stress and hard feelings.

BAD BEHAVIOR

Abuse and infidelity are never OK. If you are being abused or cheated on by a boyfriend, get out of the relationship before it destroys you. You absolutely deserve better, no matter the circumstances.

MAKING BREAKING UP EASIER

Although breaking up is never easy, it's an unavoidable component to almost every romantic relationship. Fortunately, there are some steps you can take toward making sure your breakup is as painless as possible.

DO IT IN PERSON

Because breaking up is so difficult to endure, some people find it easier to do it over the phone or in an email. However, initiating a breakup this way is considered cowardly and insensitive. Unless your soon-to-be ex has hurt you in some way, it's important to show him or her that you still care for and respect him or her by breaking up in person. Only then will your ex be able to express feelings to you and give you a proper good-bye.

DO IT IN PRIVATE

Needless to say, breaking up when other people are around can be a humiliating experience. Even if you have bad feelings about your soon-to-be ex, remember that you once had strong positive feelings for him or her. It is much more respectful to break up with someone in private.

A face-to-face breakup might feel too difficult, especially if you're angry or hurt, but you owe it to your ex to end the relationship in person.

BE HONEST

When breaking up with someone, you should never try to be hurtful. However, this doesn't mean you shouldn't be honest about why you want to end the relationship. The other person has the right to know why you feel the way you do. Some people try and lessen the pain of a breakup by making empty promises, such as, "We can still be friends." Rarely do people ever mean such things, as being friends with an ex is almost as difficult as staying in a broken relationship. During a breakup, never make a promise you don't intend to keep. The other person will become angry once he or she finds out you were being untruthful.

KEEP IT SHORT

Some couples turn a breakup conversation into a long-lasting debate. They rehash the relationship for days, weeks, or even months because they are too afraid to actually end it. With one party trying to convince the other that they can still make things work, they break up and make up over and over, forcing themselves to endure a continuous cycle of pain.

When it comes to breaking up with someone, it's best to have it over and done with as soon as possible. When a relationship is no longer working, it's impossible to put it back together again for good without a lot of hard work by both of you.

AFTER THE BREAKUP

The actual breakup conversation is, unfortunately, only part of the breakup process. After breaking up with someone, you can expect to feel pretty miserable for a while. However, you can also expect that things will get better. Although it may not seem like it at the time, it's possible to get over any breakup and be stronger for it in the end. In the meantime, here are some things you can do to lessen the pain.

- **Keep your friends around.** Unless you've become a "vanishing friend," your friends will be around to support you through a breakup. The more you hang out with them, the more fun you will have, and the less your mind will wander back to your ex and "the way things were."

- **Don't overanalyze.** It can be tempting to replay a broken relationship over and over in your head in an effort to figure out exactly what went wrong. Doing this, however, is useless. The only thing you can know for certain after a breakup is that things just didn't work out. Don't torture yourself by trying to place blame or find closure. The only way you'll feel better is if you pick yourself up and move on without looking back.

- **Stay positive.** There are positive aspects to any breakup, believe it or not. Once you're no longer part of a couple, you'll have more time for your friends. You'll also be able to reconnect with yourself and develop new hobbies and interests. And the best part is, once you're fully ready, you'll be free to meet a guy you are more compatible with.

Although romantic relationships are sometimes tough, they have plenty of positives, too. If both partners respect one another and have similar relationship goals, it can be extremely satisfying. Although no relationship is without its ups and downs, it can be a relationship that helps build you both up. Your partner can offer support through the bad times and share and revel in the good times, too.

10 GREAT QUESTIONS TO ASK A SCHOOL COUNSELOR

1. What are some signs of being in an unhealthy relationship?
2. How can I balance my relationships with my schoolwork?
3. Can you recommend any resources for dealing with an unstable relationship?
4. How can I manage the stress that comes with my relationships?
5. Are there any after-school programs where I can make new friends?
6. Do you know of any teachers who might serve as a mentor to me?
7. What are some things I can say to a friend who has fallen victim to peer pressure?
8. How can I go about seeing a therapist?
9. Do you have a list of local crisis centers?
10. How can I talk to my parents about my relationships?

CHAPTER 5

BE TRUE TO YOU

You will have all kinds of relationships in your life. But one is more important than all the rest combined: your relationship with yourself.

You can actually be two very different people. Have you ever dressed a certain way just to fit in or claimed to like a certain music group just because your friends were fans? If so, you know what it's like to not be true to yourself. In cases like these, it's as if there are two of you: the person you truly are and the person you only appear to be.

Having a healthy relationship with yourself means being true to the person you really are. If you ignore this person, you will never be fully content. No matter how popular you become or what a loving boyfriend you have, a little voice inside of you will be asking, "Hey, what about me?"

Dressing a certain way to fit in with a group is just one example of a way you have not been true to yourself.

Staying true to yourself while in high school can be tough. Often, the person you really are doesn't look or act like the people your peers look up to most. You therefore push your true self to the back of your mind, making way for a new, more socially acceptable version of yourself. Making this move is never worth it. If you put all your time and energy into being someone you're not, how will your true self ever grow and succeed?

Teens who aren't true to themselves almost always end up in trouble. In an effort to fit in, they submit to peer pressure and take on friends who don't really care about them. If they listened to their true selves more often, their futures would be much brighter. Your true self is smarter than you think. Most likely, she has better morals and aspirations than the other side of you—the person who just wants to be liked. By listening to her advice once in a while, you could be doing yourself a big favor.

You may not realize it, but even the most popular, seemingly happy teens have issues with self-esteem. Being a teenager means undergoing a period of tremendous change. Changes are rapidly occurring to your body and mind, and you have new responsibilities. It's almost impossible to be comfortable and happy with yourself when you are constantly evolving. Feeling confused or upset about your identity doesn't mean you're inadequate or unworthy. It simply means you're a normal teenager facing normal teenage problems.

TEEN GIRLS AND THEIR SELF-ESTEEM

Self-esteem, or confidence in how people view themselves and their abilities, can be a fragile thing. Low self-esteem can consume just about every aspect of someone's life, which of course can be very damaging. According to dosomething.org:

- 44 percent of high school girls are trying to lose weight.
- 70 percent of girls between the ages of fifteen and seventeen skip activities such as going to school when they feel bad about themselves.
- 75 percent of girls who have low self-esteem said that they take part in activities such as "cutting, bullying, smoking, drinking, or disordered eating." Only 25 percent of girls with high self-esteem reported taking part in such activities.
- Around 20 percent of all teenagers will battle depression before they reach adulthood.
- Teenaged girls who feel bad about themselves are four times more likely to engage in activities with boys that they later regret.
- Seven out of ten girls feel like "they are not good enough or don't measure up in some way, including their looks, performance in school and relationships with friends and family members."
- Self-esteem for girls has far more to do with how they view themselves than what they actually weigh.

Some teens have a difficult time dealing with their issues of self-esteem. They aren't sure how to develop confidence on their own, so they try and make themselves feel better by putting others down instead. This strategy never works. You may not know it to observe these people, but they usually feel pretty badly about the way they behave toward others. They therefore end up feeling even worse about themselves than they did before they started bullying.

Other teens try to boost their self-esteem by "fishing" for compliments. They say bad things about themselves in the presence of others, hoping these people will assure them they're wrong. This is another example of a useless technique for developing self-respect. No one likes to listen to someone whine and complain about themselves, so people who fish for compliments often don't accomplish more than persuading others to stay away from them.

Developing self-confidence is no easy matter, but don't think that putting other people down is the way to feel better about yourself.

BUILDING YOURSELF UP

The only person who can effectively increase your self-esteem is you. Of course, when you're so used to putting yourself down, learning to build yourself back up again can require a concentrated effort. Here are some ways in which you can retrain yourself to think positively:

- **Compliment yourself.** Admit it. You deserve a compliment once in a while. Sadly, most teens spend so much time trying to convince themselves they're not good enough that they're soon unable to recognize their many positive qualities. Next time you start to insult yourself, try paying yourself a compliment instead. A teen who didn't get the solo she wanted in the high school band may try to convince herself she's untalented. What she should do, however, is compliment herself on being brave enough to try out in the first place. Not everyone has the courage to do that. Another young woman may be upset over her low SAT score. Her first instinct may be to tell herself she's unintelligent. However, she'd be better off if she patted herself on the back for being so passionate about her academics. Her deep desire to succeed will surely help her with her studies, resulting in a higher score the next time around.

- **Refocus on the positive.** When you get home from school, instead of wincing over the bad things that happened to you that day, try making a list of the day's positive occurrences. You may be surprised to find that your time at school really wasn't as bad as you thought. If you still can't get a few negative notions out of your head, go ahead and write these down, as well. Take a look at this second list. Are the items included really worth agonizing over? If so, what can you do to improve your situation? It's no use being upset over something you're not planning on making better.

- **Have a plan.** Certain things in life take work. No one becomes a stellar student, talented artist, or impressive athlete overnight. That said, if you're motivated enough, you can absolutely achieve greatness. Rather than just sitting around wishing you possessed a certain skill, create a concrete plan outlining the steps required for achieving it. At first, your plan may seem like a huge undertaking. It's possible that you'll find it intimidating. However, once you get to work on it, before long, you'll be well on your way toward reaching your goal.

- **Survey your surroundings.** Learn to be comfortable with taking an honest look at the people you surround yourself with. Are there

Writing in a journal can be a good way to express your feelings. It can also help you work out a plan to make positive changes in your life.

friends or family members in your life who are constantly putting you down or not supporting your dreams? Your sense of self-worth may depend on your distancing yourself from such people. Remember, an uncaring relationship is never worth your time.

WHO ARE YOU?

Developing a positive relationship with your true self is all well and good, but what if you still aren't sure who that person is exactly? Again, it's normal for teenagers to not yet have a solid sense of self, so there's no reason to look down on yourself for feeling this way. In the meantime, here are some things you can do to get a better grasp on your true identity.

SPEND QUALITY ALONE TIME

Taking a look at your relationship with yourself probably isn't something you're used to doing. When you have so many other relationships to keep track of, it can be easy to forget about your own needs. Making other people happy is a noble goal, but if you don't take time for yourself, you won't have a good idea of who you really are and who you want to become.

Set aside some alone time each day and use it to further your quest for self-discovery. Listen to music, write in a journal, or simply close your eyes and relax.

No matter what solitary activity you choose to engage in, if it's all for you, you'll be one step closer to becoming acquainted with yourself.

FIND A MENTOR

A mentor is an older, more experienced person who can help you figure out your life's path. If you have a teacher, tutor, coach, or relative you look up to, ask her if she wouldn't mind talking to you about your future. Many adults would be honored to assist a younger person with her search for her true self and purpose. A mentor will share with you the lessons she's learned, mistakes she's made, and successes she's had in an effort to help you succeed. Working with a mentor will give you a better idea of what you want out of life and will consequently give you a better idea of who it is you want to be.

A mentor's experience can be a tremendous resource to help you plan your future. For example, a music teacher might help explain the pros and cons of a music career.

CONDUCT POSITIVE EXPERIMENTS

Experimenting with drugs and alcohol never yields positive results, but there are other perfectly healthy ways in which you can experiment with your image. For example, go ahead and try listening to a new type of music or dressing in a new sort of way, just to see how you like it. Neither of these activities are harmful to your health, after all. Just make sure, however, that you're experimenting for the sake of getting to know yourself rather than trying to be like someone else.

STAY ALERT

On a daily basis, pay attention to how you react to things. What memories make you smile? Which conversations hold your interest? What are the subjects you catch yourself daydreaming about? Don't allow certain things to spark your interest, only to fade from your mind a moment later. Clues about your true identity pop up all the time in everyday life, so make sure to keep an eye out for them.

Getting to know yourself should be fun, not stressful, so don't feel pressured to figure out every detail of your personality while in high school. Self-discovery is a lifelong process, especially since we undergo so many different changes as time goes on. There are certain aspects of yourself that are less likely to change, however, such as your values and morals. These aspects are especially worth paying attention to whenever you feel swayed by peer pressure.

CELEBRITIES AND THEIR MENTORS

- Media mogul Oprah Winfrey was mentored by a fourth grade teacher, Mrs. Duncan. She was also mentored later by Maya Angelou, a poet, educator, historian, best-selling author, actress, playwright, civil-rights activist, producer, and director.
- Maya Angelou was mentored by Mrs. Bertha Flowers, a woman who lived in the town where Angelou grew up.
- Actress Gwyneth Paltrow's mentor is pop superstar Madonna.
- Fox News reporter Kyung B. Yoon was mentored by major network news anchor Connie Chung.
- Facebook's chief operating (or operations) officer, Sheryl Sandberg had a mentor in her college professor Larry Summers.
- Mother Teresa found a mentor in Father Michael van der Peet.
- Actress, dancer, and singer Chita Rivera was mentored by her teacher Doris Jones.
- Physicist and astronaut Sally Ride was mentored by her professor in graduate school, Dr. Arthur Walker. He encouraged her to become an astronaut!

Having a good relationship with yourself will actually improve your other relationships. When people see that you hold yourself in high regard, they'll

Don't stress about figuring out every last detail of who you are during high school. Many people spend their whole lives discovering themselves.

be more likely to respect you. Being true to yourself will also make you a better communicator. If you know exactly what you want and how you feel, you'll have an easier time expressing yourself to others. Finally, if you love yourself the way you deserve to be loved, you'll be less likely to join up with those people who are unworthy of your time.

When it comes down to it, you—and no one else—are in control of how you feel about yourself. So don't waste your time worrying about whether or not other people accept you. If you have a good relationship with yourself, positive relationships with other people are more likely to follow.

GLOSSARY

ANCESTOR A person from whom one is descended; a distant relative.

ANCHOR The principal news spokesperson, usually in broadcasting or athletics.

ATTRIBUTE A quality or characteristic.

COMMUNICATION The exchange of thoughts, opinions, and information.

COMPROMISE An agreement reached through an adjustment of conflicting ideas.

CONUNDRUM A perplexing problem.

DICTATORSHIP A place that is ruled by one person, or a dictator.

EMPATHY Identification with and understanding of another's situation, feelings, and motives.

GENEALOGY The study of family ancestries and histories.

IDENTITY The sense of self.

IMPROVISATION Made up on the spot, such as in comedy, theatre, or music.

LGBT An abbreviation for lesbian, gay, bisexual, and transgendered people.

LOYALTY The state of being true to one's words, promises, vows, etc.

MENTOR Another person who guides someone; a mentor is usually older and has more experience.

MOGUL An extremely influential person, usually in the media or motion picture business.

MORALS Motivation based on concepts of right and wrong.

PEERS People who are equal in age, rank, or class with another or others.

PERSONA The role that one plays in public.

REHASH To go back over; to discuss again.

RELATIONSHIP A connection between people.

THERAPIST A trained professional who works with people to help them improve.

VALUES Beliefs in which you have an emotional investment.

The American School Counselor Association (ASCA)
1101 King Street, Suite 310
Alexandria, VA 22314
(800) 306-4722
Email: asca@schoolcounselor.org
Website: http://www.schoolcounselor.org
The American School Counselor Association (ASCA) supports school counselors' efforts to help students' personal/social and career development.

Family Service Toronto
Central Office
202-128A Sterling Road
Toronto, ON M6R 2B7
Canada
(416) 595-9618
Website: http://www.familyservicetoronto.org
Family Service Toronto strengthens individuals, families, and communities through counseling and education.

Girls Incorporated
120 Wall Street, 3rd Floor
New York, NY 10005
(212) 509-2000
Email: communications@girlsinc.org

Website: http://www.girlsinc.org
Girls Incorporated is a national nonprofit youth organization dedicated to inspiring all girls to be strong, smart, and bold.

National Domestic Violence Hotline
PO Box 161810
Austin, TX 78716
(800) 799-SAFE (7233)
Website: http://www.ndvh.org
The National Domestic Violence Hotline provides domestic violence crisis intervention, safety planning, information, and referrals.

The National Genealogical Society
3108 Columbia Pike, Suite 300
Arlington, VA 22204
(800) 473-0060
Email: ngs@ngsgenealogy.org
Website: http://www.ngsgenealogy.org
The National Genealogical Society promotes interest in the field of genealogy and family history.

Planned Parenthood Federation of America
Planned Parenthood of New York City, Inc.
26 Bleecker Street
New York, NY 10012
(212) 541-7800

Website: https://www.plannedparenthood.org/teens/relationships

Planned Parenthood is a resource for health care as well as all kinds of self-care for men and women, as well as young people in all kinds of relationships.

RAINN: Rape, Abuse, and Incest National Network
2000 L Street NW
Washington, DC 20036
(202) 544-3064
(800) 656-4673 (HOPE)
Website: http://www.rainn.org

RAINN is the world's largest anti-sexual assault organization. Their website offers information and support for those who are abused as well as their loved ones.

TeensHealth
c/o The Nemours Foundation
10140 Centurion Parkway North
Jacksonville, FL 32256
(904) 697-4100
Website: http://kidshealth.org/en/teens/healthy-relationship.html

TeensHealth offers information about health, emotions, and life for kids and teens in a safe, private environment.

Younger Women's Task Force
American Association of University Women (AAUW)
1310 L Street, NW, Suite 1000
Washington, DC 20005
(202) 785-7700
Website: http://www.aauw.org/membership/ywtf/
The Younger Women's Task Force is a nationwide diverse and inclusive grassroots movement dedicated to organizing younger women and their allies to take action on issues that matter most to them.

WEBSITES

Because of the changing nature of internet links, Rosen Publishing has developed an online list of websites related to the subject of this book. This site is updated regularly. Please use this link to access this list:

http://www.rosenlinks.com/WITW/relationships

FOR FURTHER READING

Anderson, Laura Halse. *Speak*. New York, NY: Square Fish, 2014.

Anthony, Maggie, and Debra Beck. *My Feet Aren't Ugly!: A Girl's Guide to Loving Herself from the Inside Out*. New York, NY: Beaufort Books, 2014.

Burmingham, Sarah O'Leary. *How to Raise Your Parents: A Teen Girl's Survival Guide*. San Francisco, CA: Chronicle Books, 2011. Ebook.

Byers, Ann. *Sexual Assault and Abuse*. New York, NY: Rosen Publishing, 2016.

Fine, Debra. *Beyond Texting: The Fine Art of Face-to-Face Communication for Teenagers*. New York, NY: Canon Publishers, 2014.

Fonda, Jane. *Being a Teen: Everything Teen Girls & Boys Should Know About Relationships, Sex, Love, Health, Identity & More*. New York, NY: Random House, 2014.

Hemmen, Lucy. *The Teen Girl's Survival Guide: Ten Tips for Making Friends, Avoiding Drama, and Coping with Social Stress*. Oakland, CA: New Harbinger Publications, 2015.

Hurt, Avery Elizabeth. *Cross-Cultural Etiquette* (Etiquette Rules!). New York, NY: Rosen Publishing, 2017.

Lang, Amy. *Dating Smarts—What Every Teen Needs to Date, Relate or Wait*. Seattle, WA: CreateSpace Independent Publishing, 2016.

Levy, Barrie. *In Love and in Danger: A Teen's Guide to Breaking Free of Abusive Relationships.* Paradise, CA: Paw Prints, 2011.

Levy, Barrie. *When Dating Becomes Dangerous: A Parent's Guide to Preventing Relationship Abuse.* Center City, MN: Hazelden, 2013.

Miles, Lisa. *How to Survive Dating.* New York, NY: Rosen Publishing, 2014.

Payment, Simone. *Friendship, Dating, and Relationships* (Teens; Being Gay, Lesbian, Bisexual, or Transgender). New York, NY: Rosen Publishing, 2010.

Skeen, Michelle, and Matthew McKay. *Communication Skills for Teens: How to Listen, Express, and Connect for Success.* Oakland, CA: New Harbinger Publications, 2016.

BIBLIOGRAPHY

Adams, Cindy. "Oprah Dishes on her Friendship with Gayle." Page Six, March 12, 2014. http://pagesix.com/2014/03/12/oprah-dishes-on-her-friendship-with-gayle/.

Bliss, Beverly. "Step Families." Parenthood in America, 1998. http://parenthood.library.wisc.edu/Bliss/Bliss.html.

CBS News. "Oprah: 'Not a better human' than Gayle King." CBS Interactive, April 2, 2012. http://www.cbsnews.com/news/oprah-not-a-better-human-than-gayle-king/.

The Center for the Study of Long Distance Relationships. "FAQs About Long Distance Relationships." 2016. http://www.longdistancerelationships.net.

"Dating the Jewish Way." Chabad-Lubavitch Media Center, 2016 http://www.chabad.org/library/article_cdo/aid/448427/jewish/Dating-the-Jewish-Way.htm.

"11 Facts About Teens and Self Esteem." DoSomething.org. Retrieved November 8, 2016. https://www.dosomething.org/us/facts/11-facts-about-teens-and-self-esteem.

Fox, Jesse David. "The History of Tina Fey and Amy Poehler's Best Friendship." Vulture, December 15, 2015. http://www.vulture.com/2013/01/history-of-tina-and-amys-best-friendship.html.

Garcia, Patricia. "12 Famous Best Friends Who Rule Hollywood," *Vogue*, February 13, 2015. http://www.vogue.com/10720911/famous-celebrity-best-friends/.

Glum, Julia. "Teen Dating Trends 2015: Technology Can Make Relationships Closer But Facilitate Abuse, Report Finds." International Business Times, October 1, 2015. http://www.ibtimes.com/teen-dating-trends-2015-technology-can-make-relationships-closer-facilitate-abuse-212273.

Kimble, Lindsay. "Tina Fey and Amy Poehler On Their Decades-Spanning Friendship: We're 'Found' Sisters." *People*, December 1, 2015. http://people.com/movies/tina-fey-and-amy-poehler-on-their-decades-spanning-friendship.

Kuff, Nicolette. "New Survey Reveals Alarming Statistics Related to Teen Relationships and Abuse." Blogger News Network, July 26, 2008. http://www.bloggernews.net/116921.

Lenhart, Amanda, Monica Anderson, and Aaron Smith. "Teens, Technology, and Romantic Relationships." Pew Research Center, October 1, 2015. http://www.pewinternet.org/2015/10/01/teens-technology-and-romantic-relationships/.

Mahdi, Ali Akbar. "Fending for Themselves." The Iranian, August 1, 2003. http://www.iranian.com/AliAkbarMahdi/2003/August/Book/.

Penn, Charli. "Girlfriends: Oprah Winfrey and Gayle King's Friendship Through the Years." *Essence*, February, 19, 2013. http://www.essence.com/galleries/girlfriends-oprah-winfrey-and-gayle-kings-friendship-through-years.

Peterson, Karen. "Teenage Girls Setting Boundaries in Relationships, Sex." *USA Today*, April 22, 2002. http://www.usatoday.com/news/health/child/2002-04-23-teen-sex.htm.

Rhodes, Jean. "Top 25 Mentoring Relationships in History." The Chronicle of Evidence-Based Mentoring, September 13, 2015. http://chronicle.umbmentoring.org/top-25-mentoring-relationships-in-history/.

Study Guides and Strategies. "Active Listening." Retrieved November 13, 2016. http://www.studygs.net/listening.htm.

INDEX

ABOUT THE AUTHORS

Zoe Lowery is an avid student of history, with a particular interest in women's roles. When she's not writing or editing, Lowery enjoys experimenting with recipes in the kitchen or riding her motorcycle over the mountains or to her local library in Colorado.

Bethany Bezdecheck is a writer and nonprofit professional living in the New York City area with her husband and dog. Her current passions include politics, bunny rabbits, independent films, artisan cheeses, jewelry making, and learning to speak Romanian.

PHOTO CREDITS

Cover oliveromg/Shutterstock.com; p. 7 Cooper Neill/Getty Images; p. 11 Kevin Winter/Getty Images; p. 16 RyanKing999/iStock/Thinkstock; p. 19 monkeybusinessimages/iStock/Thinkstock; pp. 20–21 g-stockstudio/iStock/Thinkstock; p. 25 DragonImages/iStock/Thinkstock; pp. 28–29 gpointstudio/iStock/Thinkstock; p. 31 digitalskillet/iStock/Thinkstock; pp. 32–33 Cole_21/iStock/Thinkstock; p. 37 Pixland/Thinkstock; pp. 42–43 massimofusaro/iStock/Thinkstock; pp. 44–45 JackF/iStock/Thinkstock; pp. 46–47 CREATISTA/iStock/Thinkstock; pp. 48–49 Purestock/Thinkstock; p. 53 theprint/iStock/Thinkstock; p. 55 Jupiterimages/Stockbyte/Thinkstock; p. 57 Martin Novak/Shutterstock.com; p. 61 Wavebreakmedia Ltd/Thinkstock; pp. 64–65 Astarot/iStock/Thinkstock; p. 67 gdjukanovic/iStock/Thinkstock; pp. 70–71 mihtiander/iStock/Thinkstock; pp. 72–73 Marjan_Apostolovic/iStock/Thinkstock; p. 77 Feverpitched/iStock/Thinkstock; p. 83 MilanMarkovic/iStock/Thinkstock; pp. 86–87 Wavebreakmedia/iStock/Thinkstock; p. 90 AndreyPopov/iStock/Thinkstock; pp. 92–93, 96 michaeljung/iStock/Thinkstock; cover and interior pages background designs lulias/Shutterstock.com, Dawid Lech/Shutterstock.com, Transia Design/Shutterstock.com.

Designer: Nicole Russo-Duca